Livewell
Lead meaningful Life

Sanket Prasade
Meghana Prasade

First published in 2018 by

Becomeshakespeare.com
Wordit Content Design & Editing Services Pvt Ltd
Unit - 26, Building A-1, Nr Wadala RTO,
Wadala (East),
Mumbai 400037, India
T:+91 8080226699

Copyright © 2018 by Sanket Prasade and Meghana Prasade

All rights reserved. Any unauthorized reprint or use of this material is prohibited. No part of this book may be reproduced or transmitted in any form or by any means, electronic or mechanical, including photocopying, recording, or by any information storage and retrieval system without express written permission from the author/publisher.
Please do not participate in or encourage piracy of copyrighted materials in violation of the author's rights. Purchase only authorized editions.

©
ISBN: 978-93-86487-89-6

Acknowledgement

I would like to dedicate this book to my mother, Late Mrs. Vasudha Prasade. She has always been my biggest support system and we all dearly miss her.

Writing this book would have been impossible without my wife, Meghana Prasade, who motivated me and helped me to complete and publish it.

I would also take this opportunity to thank our mentor, Dr. Arun Mishra who inspired us to write our own book and motivated us to begin a new innings in our lives.

This journey towards fitness and starting a business of our own, is also greatly inspired by our spiritual guru, Dr. Avanii Rajyadhashya, and our business guru, Mr. Atul Rajoli. Without their guidance and unconditional support, all our attempts at success would have been in vain. This idea was completely new to us.

I would also like to thank you, dear readers, for taking the time from your busy lives to read and acknowledge our book.

Summary

This is an inspirational tell-all book written by Sanket Prasade and his wife, Meghana Prasade. 'Livewell - Lead Meaningful Life', follows the couple's transformation from fat to fit. While reading the book you will realize that it is only you who can make a difference in your life. This book will also teach you self-acceptance and ways to increase confidence. It speaks in detail about the connection of the mind and the body; and how it influences your thoughts, attitude, and beliefs. Reading this book will undoubtedly inspire you to undergo a mental as well as a physical transformation, and to become a better human being.

Dear Sanket & Meghana,

Many Many Congratulations on your first book. I am so proud of whatever you have achieved, right from physical fitness to spiritual fitness.

The best part about you both is that you do not only have the conventional nutritional angle to your plans but you take care of the emotional, mental & spiritual fitness as well.

You are one of those students who have been very creative, curious and sincere. I still remember the discussion about nutrition we had for the first time and I was very impressed with the way you conceived your knowledge.

Each and every thought is a prayer and it is energy. The energy then transforms into cells in your body. The body being a universal being it does not acknowledge the cells having negative energy. So, the cells formed with the energy of thought like revenge, jealousy, hatred, etc. are not accepted by the body and thus they form a dis-ease in the body which we know as 'disease' or 'sickness.' This is exactly where you; Sanket & Meghana are different from the other wellness coach available.

What I like about you is that you will not only give the correct diet and health help but also the perfect health counselling with the emotional and physical body. Your affirmations and prayers work wonders!

All my best wishes to the both of you and I am happy for our association.

Regards,

Avanii R

Dr. Avanii Deepak Rajadhyaksha

PhD. Hon. (A.M.)

M. D. (A.M.)

- Founder, Infinite Healing™

LAKSHYAVEDH
INSTITUTE OF LEADERSHIP AND EXCELLENCE
Empowering Life

Dear Sanket & Meghna Prasade,

I know Sanket and Meghana Prasade for quite some time now, and I am really proud about the fact that both of them are LAKSHYAVEDHIS. Initially when I met both of them they both narrated their own transformational experience of going from overweight and unhealthy lifestyle to fit and healthy life. I was very much impressed by their story.

They both came to LAKSHYAVEDH to grow professionally. I was so amazed to see their commitment towards LAKSHYAVEDH FOUNDATION and LAKSHYAVEDH INTERMEDIATE Training Programs. They are very passionate about adding value to people's lives and helping others to lead meaningful life. I have personally seen their dedication towards their mission. Now I am even more happy to see that they are coming up with this informative and important book about how one can live a meaningful life in terms of his mind and body. It will definitely make a difference to thousands of people for sure.

I wish them both all the very best. Keep on adding value to lives of people..!!

Just do it!

LAKSHYAVEDHI ATUL RAJOLI

Contents

1. Importance of health 9
2. Importance of mental health 13
3. Connection between mind and body 16
4. Benefits of mental and physical transformation 21
5. Connection between financial health and physical health 28
6. Our Physical transformation 33
7. Life changing transformation 50
8. Meet our Mentor 54
9. Career opportunity 59
10. Formation of the Company 62
11. Our services 85

1

Importance of health

Health is wealth, it is often stated. Good and adequate nutrition in your diet is a very important part of leading a Healthy Life, along with efficient and regular physical activities. These help you to reach and maintain a healthy weight, to reduce the risk of diseases, and to retain overall health. Being healthy is essential as it helps maintain a stronger heart, better muscles, stronger bones, a sense of wellbeing, and a better social life.

We are taught many useful things in school, but all of this gets lost somewhere in our mad rush to earn a degree and get a job. Our connect with exercise disappears and infrequent eating patterns make us overweight. My wife and I went through the same. This prompted us to look out for exercise in the year 2014.

Livewell

Importance of health

Physical as well as mental health has an immediate influence on our daily routine. It is entirely in our own hands to maintain good health. It is not something that is sold in a store but something that we must create through single-minded determination and toil; and endeavor to maintain it always.

If we follow a few simple steps in our day-to-day lives, we will realize the importance of having a healthy lifestyle. It will not only add benefits to daily living but will also make you professionally successful. Following a healthy diet every day will help reduce lifestyle-related illness, which in turn saves a lot of money usually spent on treatments and medication.

Sickness and good health are the two sides of the same coin. Whenever there is a slight change in our daily routine, there is imbalance happens internally and externally. It is therefore important to maintain regularity as an essential element to sustaining good physical and mental health in one's life.

Livewell

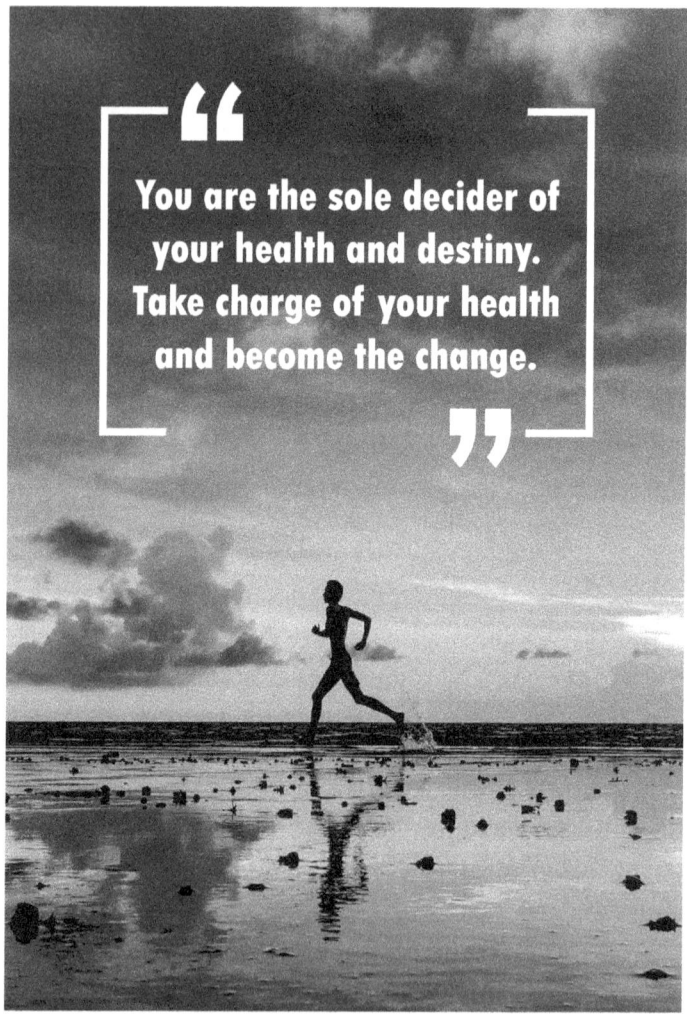

2

Importance of mental health

Mental health includes the day-to-day emotions that we face in our personal and professional lives. It directly affects our thought process, belief systems, and our daily actions. It also helps us to determine how to handle stress and make reasonable choices. Balanced mental health is very essential at every stage of our life — from childhood to old age.

Imbalanced mental health, on the other hand, directly leads to, low or no energy to work; withdrawing from people and daily work activities; eating or sleeping, too much or too little; and feeling helpless and hopeless. These are some of the symptoms of mental illness or low-level mental health.

Now the question is, why should we maintain a positive mental health balance in our daily routine?

Livewell

Importance of mental health

The reason is that, positive thoughts or good mental health helps us realize our inner potentials, cope better with stress, improve work productivity, and make meaningful contributions to the society.

But somewhere in our day-to-day lives, we fail to maintain our mental and physical health balance and that's when troubles creep in. I am sharing this because, not so long ago, I was 20 kg overweight and suffering from tremendous physical and mental stress.

And as I have mentioned earlier, your own thoughts or mental health directly impact your physical health. Positive mental-health-balance helps you to connect with other people in a better way, have a positive mindset, and be more physically active.

There is a very strong connection between the mind and the body. Any kind of physical pain will directly affect our day, our daily work and our time with the family. It has a direct link to stress, depression, and a low immune system, which can seriously affect our performance.

3

Connection between mind and body

If you have good emotional health, you will always be aware of your thoughts, feelings and behaviour. You will always come up with healthy solutions for any stress or other problems that are normal in our day-to-day existence. You will always feel good about yourself and have healthy relationships in your personal and professional lives.

There are several disturbing moments that directly affect our emotional health daily, and can lead to strong feelings of sadness and anxiety. Always remember that your body responds to the way you think, which we call "body and mind connection". When you are stressed or upset, the body reacts in a way that might indicate something is wrong. Poor emotional health can be a cause for the body's weak immune system. Also, when you are feeling stressed

Connection between mind and body

or upset, you may not take the time to care for your health physically and mentally, which usually results in impulse eating and procrastination of daily tasks.

Eating right and doing the right amount of exercise, will lead to better physical and mental health overall.

That's why you must always take care of yourself. To have good emotional health, it is very important to take good care of your body by having regular healthy meals; getting enough sleep, i.e., 7 to 8 hours a day; and most importantly, exercising at least five days a week. If you want to achieve a good mind and body balance then it is very important to set a health goal and to set yourself to achieving a little every day. You need to work out and eat nutritious food rich in proteins, vitamins, fiber, and minerals. If you want to change yourself, start by changing your mind and your body will follow, and that in turn will automatically shape your thoughts.

Livewell

Connection between mind and body

Our mind and body are closely linked to each other; their relationship can exert a positive effect on our health and quality of life.

Our thoughts play a central role and if there is an awareness of the mind and body connection, then it may improve the quality of life. The mind-body connection helps fight stress, especially during an illness. In the case of any injury or disease, medicines do play an important role, but if we maintain a positive attitude the results will be maximum.

Our mind and emotions are directly connected to our health and by understanding this relationship we can play a greater role in maintaining our wellbeing. We often overlook connection because of our busy schedules. Imagine, a machine is not working properly and is making noises. What do we do? We repair it. Similarly, if we ignore our health, our body informs us of any malfunction through stress or illness. You can change parts of a functional machine but your body parts cannot be changed. If there is a proper two-way communication between the mind and the body, then it will have positive affects on our physical, mental, and emotional health. Your body always speaks your mind.

Here I want to share that our mind consists of various mental states like, thoughts, emotions, beliefs, attitudes and images. The brain is the main hardware that allows our body to experience these mental states. You must therefore be aware of the mind and body connection. Livewell is ready to help you balance this connection with various simple techniques.

Three years ago my mind pushed me to hunt for a wellness coach in order to control my excess weight. Ridding myself of the surplus weight has made it easier for me to maintain my mind and body connection with the help of an easy plan right in the midst my busy work schedule.

Make rules for yourself and follow them strictly. Always respect your mind and body, only then will the two help you back.

4

Benefits of mental and physical transformation

Mental and physical transformation improves our concentration and focus. It helps us face stress and worry and reduces irritation, anger, and frustration. It helps improve inner peace and happiness, which directly impacts our personal and professional lives. Mental and physical strength increases confidence and self-esteem towards any challenge that we may face in our day-to-day life. It allows for a positive outlook on life and relationships. This transformation gives us the courage to handle any situation in life.

But sometimes obstacles come in the way and I have found that results or excuses are the two things that never work at the same time. You can either have results or you can have excuses, but not both. To change things around you, it is *you* who has to change first.

A) *Time*: This is the most common fitness excuse of them all. Replace one hour a day, throughout the week, of watching TV, surfing the web and chatting on the mobile as the first step towards being healthy. It takes only 4 per cent of your whole day! Avoid asking yourself how much time you are going to waste by exercising 1 hour/day; instead, ask yourself how much of your life you are going to waste by being mentally and physically unfit. This is the right time to take a decision for your health.

B) *Exhaustion*: Of course everybody gets exhausted, but believe it or not exercise always boosts your energy level. If you miss exercise, proper nutrition, and 8 hours of sound sleep one day, you are likely to miss the same the next day. If not controlled, it will activate your mental and physical problems. The biggest journey always begins with one small step. This is absolutely essential for our good health.

C) *My day-to-day work counts as my exercise*: This is a common mistake. The only way that your job counts as an exercise is if you are a gym instructor, a personal trainer, or a yoga teacher who works out and sweats daily with his or her clients. Walking to work or doing field-work doesn't count as exercise.

D) *Never see any results*: I am very sorry to say, but this is a very common excuse. As per my view, you don't see the expected results because —

   a) lack of regular exercise, b) eating junk food, which cancels out any workout, and c) expecting results too soon. When you start any weight management programme, you have to be very patient and wait for at least 3 months to see any mental and physical results. You should strictly follow all necessary steps for your good health .

Livewell

> Mind and body are two parts of the same soul. Your body succeeds only when your mind thrives on positivity. Your body will follow only when your mind is strong.

Benefits of mental and physical transformation

E) *I have to look after my kids*: Many times people struggle to manage their mental and physical fitness if there are kids to take care of. Combine the two. Find a play ground and take a walk around it while the kids play with their friends. You can play with them or do some fun activities with them. There are so many other ways to exercise with your kids in a playground. Your kids can be your biggest reason to exercise and not make excuses. The only limit is your imagination. Go cycling with your kids, play badminton with them, or just take a walk with them in your own building compound. When parents are fit, the family has more energy to do personal and professional activities.

F) *Less motivation*: One of the major problems faced by people is low motivation. You must first note what is keeping you away from, following a proper exercise routine, adopting correct food habits, and getting sound sleep. Everyone needs to set their own short-term and long-term goals for their own health and to live well — to maintain, gain, or to lose weight. Try to be specific about your health goals and write them down where you will catch sight of them every day. Livewell is here to motivate you at every step.

G) *I don't like to move*: First and foremost, find out why. Is it that you do not like to sweat? You can workout indoors, with air-conditioning. You can register yourself for swimming, so you don't notice the perspiration. You can do low-sweat activities like gentle forms of yoga. Is it that you are self-conscious about your excess weight? You can always start with easy exercises, i.e., start walking or exercising with a trainer who can give you personal attention and support. Always wear clothes that you feel comfortable in.

H) *I have tried exercise before*: Set goals that are small and realistic. You will only achieve success and not failure. Having an exercise buddy always keeps you accountable as well. You are more likely to show up for your workout if you know that someone is expecting you to be there. Livewell is committed to help you achieve better health. You may have tried before, but now through this book you will learn how I reduced my weight and am living a healthy life today. There is always hope and we are here to help make you physically and mentally fit.

Benefits of mental and physical transformation

> **It is not how much you eat, but how you eat and what you eat. Your food should reflect you and become your greatest asset.**

5

Connection between financial health and physical health

Regarding our own health, I think we can all agree that money is nothing without our well-being. When our health is absent, then our wealth is useless. The relationship between our finance, health status, and behavior is very strong. First of all, unhealthy choices are expensive. If you are overweight, then there are higher chances that you are spending more money on unhealthy food. This means in the future you will be facing more expenses due to your weight condition.

If you don't take care of yourself now, your health problems will cause financial problems in the future. Health stress can cause anxiety, migraine, and other physical problems, which result in heavy

Connection between financial health and physical health

medical bills. Your own physical health is achieved by being fit and healthy through exercise and proper nutrition, which reduces the contraction and occurrence of sickness and diseases. Out of physical, emotional, social, intellectual, spiritual and environmental health, physical health is the most visible.

Skipping meals or over-eating do not show immediate side-effects, but will definitely hinder your health and lifestyle later on. Over time this can lead to bigger and costlier health issues, which can produce ever greater financial distress with disastrous results.

If you allow it, your money can certainly help you improve and maintain your health properly. Poor health cuts your life short. Too much focus on earning money by skipping meals continuously can be deadly. Protect your health first. Always be responsible for your bright future and your physical well-being by exercising, eating the right food, taking time to unwind, and enjoy the life you want — in short, stop and smell the roses often.

Those who give value to a bright future and are strong enough to put money aside are more likely to also make healthier choices in the present. Many companies nowadays believe that employees can focus on their work only if the employee's health is in good condition, and therefore they should invest enough money for their own health. You should focus on managing health and taking part in financial advisory programmes at the same time. Healthy finance and healthy lifestyle always walk hand in hand. If your bank account and budget are in good shape, then there is a chance that your health is in pretty good shape too.

Being healthy financially and personally requires you to be organized with no excuses. Just like you always need to be organized with your finances, you also need to manage your food habits and fitness. Scheduling your workout requires discipline. A healthy lifestyle always pays dividends in terms of a long life. If you eat healthy and workout regularly, you keep sickness at bay, which directly connects to lack of medical bills.

In fact, structured exercise routines and regulated eating habits help to reduce the risk of diseases that directly affect your financial health in terms of prolonged medical treatments. Hence you save some big money on doctor visits and medications. I feel, a person with a strong financial background will be less stressed about any health budget than someone without one. This stress can be

Connection between financial health and physical health

a killer if you are not careful in terms of your own health. Excessive stress can lead to all sorts of unwanted conditions like depression and obesity. By eating high fiber and high protein foods daily, one can easily control untimely hunger and avoid spending unnecessary money on snacks and junk food.

Fiber, protein, vitamins, and minerals are very powerful nutrients that fill you up throughout the day and provide you with a number of benefits for your digestive and cardiovascular systems. This is usually absent in fast foods. Eating and spending money on these rich nutrients is a better way to control hunger and reduce wastage of wealth on unnecessary foods.

The correct foundation to good, healthy living is to choose food products that are rich in nutrients and have a balanced amount of vitamins, minerals, proteins, carbohydrates and a little bit of fat as well, which are essential requirements for any human being. If you choose your foods wisely, you will be able to enjoy the experience of eating, a strong immune system, and balanced physical and mental health.

A healthy you will automatically lead to a healthy monetary status. You might even skip your local supermarket and go organic. These options may be costlier, but the difference in food quality is like day and night. Eating healthy may cost you money today, but eating unhealthy can cost you your life tomorrow.

6

Our Physical transformation

Now I will elaborate on the transformation of our lives.

In the year 2014 I was hunting for a counselor to help with my wife's excess weight. She had put on a lot of weight after the birth of our son. I was looking for a gym or any other weight management center in our area. Then my father found a health center very close to our residence. I went there immediately to enquire about the weight management programme with the counselor. After a long discussion, I was convinced of their system and of the results they would deliver to their clients. On the same evening, my wife accompanied me to the center once she returned from her office. Both of us did a weight check up and she found her weight to be 73kgs, which was 19kgs in excess of her actual weight as per the standard height to weight ratio. She was at a higher risk of developing chronic illnesses.

The counselor explained the matter to us in a very simple way. She described the weight management plan and how it would work on our bodies throughout the process. Here I want to share that when I did my weight checkup along with my wife, I was shocked to find that I was 14kgs more than the weight suggested by the WHO (World Health Organization) chart. The counselor told me to start the weight transformation as well. But since I was doing my exercise very well, I thought I could do it by myself without any counseling. My belief system suggested to me that I was fit and fine. So I asked the health counselor to begin with my wife's weight transformation, as she needed it more urgently.

My wife was convinced about the weight transformation programme, because she believed in the counselor more than she believed in me. She told me she would prove that weight transformation was possible if you believed in it. At that time there was no proper eating or sleeping or exercise routine, so I doubted her confidence in the challenge.

She started her programme with proper guidance while managing her busy schedule. In only 30 days she lost 3kgs. She gained immense confidence in the process because she was on the path towards a life transformation, physically and mentally. She was determined to become better and continued for the next six months.

I also supported her decision. At that time we were both busy in our respective jobs and I felt that since it was her first month, she was on a high level of motivation; and the second month would see everything go back to normal, like the old days, because after all she was still 16kgs.overweight.

Her counselor had also gone through the same experience when she was in the process of reducing 22kgs.of excess weight. She supported my wife a lot and also gave her huge motivation. She introduced my wife to very simple diet tricks and my wife firmly believed that she was going to be transformed only because of her counselor. The counselor stressed on the point that this was not a quick process but a long journey of both physical and mental transformation.

And for this journey, Meghana got ready to wear the shoes of discipline — like, sleeping on time, eating correctly and timely, regular walking, etc. She was committed to herself and to her counselor. But I was still doubtful for her —I wanted to see how far she could go on this path of conscious discipline for body and mind transformation. The main thing about the programme was that she needed to do it on her own along with balancing her busy 10-hourwork schedule, waking up early in the morning and looking after our 2-year old son.

But thanks to her counselor's simple steps and explainations, she was able to accomplish this well. She also helped Meghana with some exercises that could be done at home. With the help of all this additional knowledge and proper nutrient intake, my wife started her journey on a high.

Here I want to share one more thing that her counselor said to her — that it was a personal journey, and a wellness counselor or guide could only help you achieve the respected goal if all rules were followed. Every month my wife was supposed to meet her to track the transformation. In this process, she got weekly feedback from her counselor about the progress, and had her queries answered. Meghana clearly understood that the journey was not easy but was possible with proper guidance.

Now Meghana had a clear idea about how to follow the rules. She realized that for good health, she must follow nature's rule as everything was linked to each other, i.e., our mind and body.

Another curious point about the programme was that she not only transformed physically but mentally as well. It was just like our initial school days when we needed to adjust to a new environment and had a lot of questions. Her counselor explained everything to Meghana and gave her lots of motivation to reach the target.

When we start anything new, as a human beings, our mind raises many questions. In school we were helped and guided by our teachers while in our personal lives, parents always came forward to help us resolve our day-to-day issues. In this case Meghana's counselor helped and motivated her through every step of her physical transformation. This is how Meghana gained so much confidence in her journey. I was watching this change in Meghana very closely and one day she insisted that I do the programme with her.

When Meghana asked me to do the programme, I told her I did not need it because I was fit and didn't have any physical and mental issues. Meghana's counselor told her that in the first month toxins are removed and thrown out of the body. In this process, the body goes through numerous changes internally which can be felt and noticed only by the individual and not by others. One more thing her counselor told her was that the weight transformation programme worked only on the excess body fat, which was the main reason behind excessive weight gain. This fat reduction helped the person reduce the risk of developing lifestyle diseases. The first month is very crucial for everyone as the mind observes these changes and reacts to them. I am very glad to state that her counselor helped her through every confusion and now Meghana was ready to enter her 2nd month.

Second Month:

Meghana's second month started on a positive note because of the 3kgs.she had lost in the first month and of course, the constant motivation from her counselor. In this process, she started to consciously avoid junk food and started eating healthy foods like salads, fruits, fresh homemade fruit juices, boiled eggs, and sprouts, which helped her gain a lot of energy while managing her hectic job schedule. In these 30 days she developed confidence in eating right. In the market there is a large variety of foods available, from junk foods to organic foods. But there is nobody to help you choose correctly. Meghana realized that the excess weight gain happened to a large extent due to her wrong food habits and breaking nature's cycle.

Our Physical transformation

In the second month her confidence level increased as she felt very energetic. Before this programme she would get easily tired while going about her daily work. But during the transformation her body started supporting her and she rarely felt tired. This rejuvenation began with the removal of all bad habits and toxins from her body and mind. And this was very necessary to transport the body to the next level. We noticed that with healthy, organic food the body automatically and positively responded to change.

In the second month, both of us went to the counselor's office for the personal counseling session. Meghana did her weight checkup and amazingly her weight had reduced another 4kgs. So now the total weight loss was 7kgs. This happened only because of proper eating habits and conscious efforts towards the transformation of her body and mind.

She insisted that I should join the programme with her, seeing the amazing results, but again I refused because I thought I was fit and fine. Even after my wife lost over 7kgs, I was convinced that I could start the process myself despite being 15kgs overweight. In those two months, Meghana followed every instruction of her health counselor. She started going for regular walks, consumed adequate amounts of water and high quality organic foods, salads, fruits, and tried to get 7 to 8 hours of sleep at night. Now her brain was perfectly programmed for good habits.

The initial stage was difficult for her but her strong commitment towards wanting a healthy lifestyle gave her a positive result. This is no miracle, it happens everywhere. But most of us aren't ready to be one of those marching towards the change. Meghana's transformation was happening in front of me, but my mind didn't allow me to engage in the process because I wanted to see her get rid of all the weight. Take a step towards healthy living, it doesn't cost much.

Just like in our profession we do various assignments and projects through hard work and commitment, this body transformation is also like an assignment where you need to give your 100%. If suppose at work we ignore a valuable project directly connected to our grand recognition and promotion, then will we get that appreciation? No! The same thing is true for your health too. If you want recognition for your attractive personality from your loved ones, then you should start the body and mind transformation at the right time. Don't do the wait

Our Physical transformation

and watch duty. Sometimes people ask others, is it working? But maybe that person did not follow the instructions properly and that's why he/she didn't get the results expected. Many people say, I tried it but it never gave me any results. Every person is unique. So for your health, you need to start and not listen to what others say.

Third Month:

By this month her unhealthy food habits had completely vanished. For the first two months she faced issues with adapting to new eating habits but now, the healthy organic food habit was in full swing. I was amazed to see her gradually transform and convert to a healthy lifestyle.

Here my exercise was also in full swing. I decided to compete with Meghana and also show her my commitment. And I was right. My belief was that I was now more fit than before. Meghana had started healthy lunch box too. In her office she walked whenever possible. She started drinking lots of water even though she knew that her toilet visits would increase in order to flush out the excess water from her body. She started regular morning and evening walks, and never used the excuse of our 2-year old son. She started to walk and play with him whenever possible, which she never did earlier, proactively and consciously.

Every morning she used to take a low calorie and high protein, high fiber breakfast; a heavy lunch in the afternoon; and less food in the evening.

In the first two months she faced some difficulties in following the programme. Even with that she successfully reduced 7kgs. due to her firm belief in the system and in her counselor.

The third month's one-on-one counseling day was very close and Meghana was confident about her performance and result. She was absolutely sure that there would be another 3 to 4kgs weight reduction. I was really surprised to see her this way. And when she did her weight checkup, the machine showed her to be another 3.5kgs lighter. Her total weight reduction at the end of the third month was 10.5kgs.

Her skin had also begun to glow and look healthy. She lost around 3kgs every month with the help of proper food habits and simple health tips from her counselor. Here she just followed nature's rule. She did this 10.5kgs weight reduction with her hectic work schedule and without any excuses. If your belief system is strong then everything is possible in your life, without any distractions. Once again she insisted that I join the programme with her, but I wanted to see the total weight transformation. I ignored her proposal.

Her counselor also insisted that I do the programme with my wife, now that I could see a living example in front of me. She made me do a weight checkup and when I stood on the weighing scale, it read 80kgs. But I still refused to do it. I told the counselor that the extra 16kgs was not a big issue for me. My fat level was 30%, but I was still not ready to change myself mentally and physically. She explained to me the reasons of weight gain even through regular exercise.

But I was adamant about seeing Meghana's transformation. Here I became an observer. My mind said, I do not have any problems today so why should I start now? If anything happened, then we would see. First, let's see what happened to Meghana.

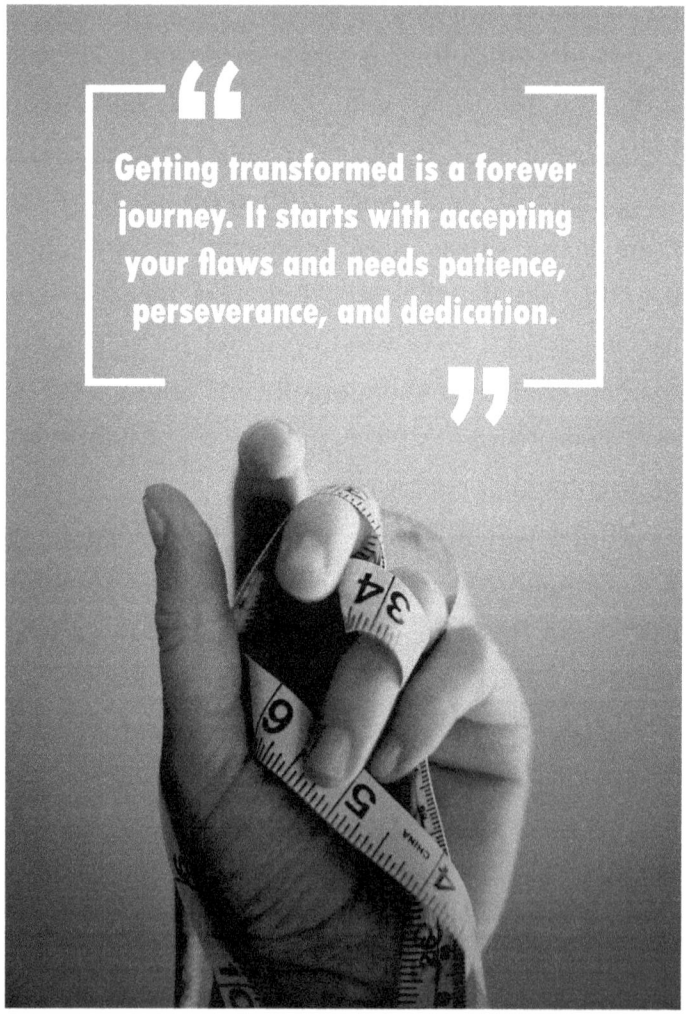

Fourth Month:

Meghana was thrilled about her result. She realized how proper nutrition could help our bodies and why it was so important to live a healthy lifestyle. She felt very energetic and noticed her body and mind remake themselves. This was her 4th month. Due to her 10.5kgs weight reduction her skin looked young and radiant. She understood well how to live healthy and energetic.

In our daily routine we see lots of food items around us. These foods include fast food, fruits, vegetables, juices, etc. But if you really want a healthy lifestyle then you need to choose your own food on a daily basis. Here I want to share one more thing; we are what we are because of our own life decisions. If today I am overweight, obese, or unhealthy, then I am the only person who is responsible for it. So if you have any desire to live a meaningful life then you have to take charge of your life and live healthy.

For this, your belief system should be strong. And this belief system will strengthen only when you see positive results. For positive results, you have to start with the good habits. That is what happened with me when I saw my wife's result after 4 months.

Livewell

We went to the counselor for Meghana's weight checkup and when she checked her weight on the machine, it showed 4gs less than the previous month's numbers. Now her total weight reduction was 14.5gs. And out of curiosity I checked my weight and it was 84kgs, 20 kgs more than my ideal body weight. Here I was told that weight reflected 80% of our eating habits and 20% of our workout. My workout was fine but there was a big issue with my diet, which was 80% of our whole day.

Meghana's weight was now 58.5gs. I realized how I had underestimated Meghana in the last 4 months. This time when Meghana asked me to start the programme, I did. I remembered being condescending in the beginning.

The same day I committed myself to a healthy lifestyle. My belief system totally changed. I realized my mistake and started to follow Meghana's counselor's instructions. Her counselor explained that the results are slow in the first three months because mental health is also in the process of transforming itself. Meghana's belief system was a proof of her transformation and could easily adapt to the physical change. Her mind was also clear about instructions for a healthy lifestyle. Now she could easily differentiate between what was right and wrong for maintaining superior physical and mental health.

Fifth and Sixth Months:

My wife started giving me instructions on how to follow the programme. — These were very simple steps that had been given by her counselor.

I started my transformation like Meghana had 4 months back. I began with a healthy breakfast in the morning that was low in calories and high in protein, fiber, vitamins, and minerals. I started to drink a lot of water throughout the day. I continued with my usual exercise regime. Meghana followed everything properly and was only 4.5kgs away from her goal.

If your belief says that something is going to happen with you, then it will definitely happen. Meghana believed her counselor's advice and started the programme. My own belief system took 4 months to realize the effectiveness of the same.

Meghana's 5th month's counseling was close, which meant I was going for my 1st. My dear friends, here I want to tell you that when I started this programme I remembered all the words that Meghana had shared with me in her first month — Ohh!!! It's amazing, it's a very nice programme;

I will definitely do this programme because I am feeling very happy and energetic.

I felt all these emotions when I began this process. I felt very similar to what Meghana had felt, and I was also rather curious about my first counseling. I felt quite sure about the result, because if she could do this then so could I. This is exactly what happens in our lives —we first watch others for results, and only then start believing in something. We say, let him or her try it, and if the results are positive, I will take a shot at it too.

We want solutions to our difficulties, but we waste our time waiting for others to show us the outcome. Opportunity comes anytime and anywhere, it is for us to grab it in time. In my case, the opportunity came with Meghana when I was already 14kgs overweight and after a wait of 4 months, I landed up with 6kgs more. Something had been missing. Meghana's counselor helped her and me.

Now in her 5th month, with 19kgs weight reduction, Meghana saw a drastic change in her mind and body. It was a proud moment for her. Amazingly, I reduced 3.5kgs in the first month with the help of simple health tips. Meghana was almost done with her physical and mental transformation

Our Physical transformation

and started to guide me through the programme, without affecting my daily work schedule. In my second month I reduced a total of 7kgs.

These results are not typical. Individual results will vary."

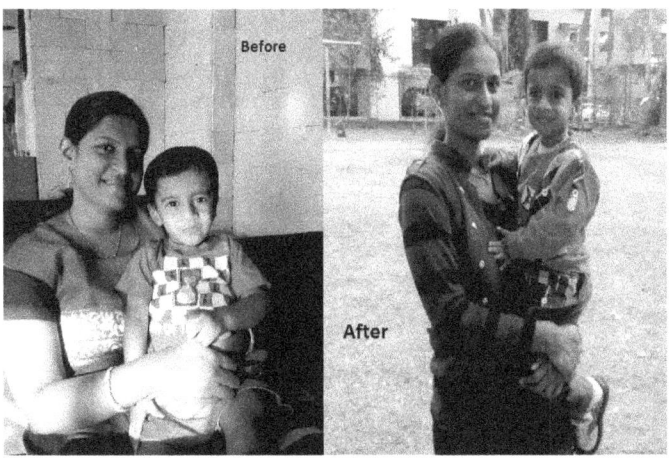

"These results are not typical. Individual results will vary."

7

Life changing transformation

(*Disclaimer*: This is our personal choice to aid others with the help of our experience and results)

Meghana attained full body transformation over a period of six months and I began to feel transformed with my 7kgs weight reduction. In our locality and work place everyone was started to ask us about the change, especially Meghana. This was a turning point for both of us. Many people wanted to know how Meghana had reduced so much weight; they wanted to know the procedure.

But here we were stumped. We did not have counseling experience or any idea about dealing with others, as every person has their own causes and symptoms.

So we decided to discuss the situation with our counselor. The first thing she said was not to worry. She told us that it was very easy to deal with people

Life changing transformation

when they asked about the transformation and that she would train us regarding the same.

She advised us to come to her office for extra learning so that we could help other people in terms of their physical and mental transformation. She taught us about the entire procedure from day 1 till the end of the process for every type of person. We were both ready and keen to do this because after our own experience we felt we could successfully assist others. We believed our counselor's words — it is so simple to help others; helping people to achieve their health goal will give you lots of blessing.

We are so thankful to our counselor for changing our lives physically and mentally.

Life changing transformation

We were both excited to help others with our counselor's guidance. She explained everything in very simple language. She told us to find out why the person wanted to get transformed, only then could we counsel them. Another thing we both learned from this was that helping others is the most joyful thing in the world — you will get appreciation, comments and blessings.

In this procedure we both received 100% support from our counselor. This was my 3rd month and my total weight reduction was around 10kgs. The feeling was great inside and out and I understood how Meghana felt in her first 3 months, and how I rejected her every proposal. I also understood that if you break nature's circle then nature will punish you, but if you follow the simple health rules then it will help you choose a healthy lifestyle. Both of us were ready to help others in our family and friend circle.

8

Meet our Mentor

This was my 4th month. Meghana was doing extremely well maintaining her reduced weight at the same level. We were both doing very well on our personal mental and physical maintenance. Our interaction with our counselor got more personal and more frequent than ever before.

In the course of our many meetings and conversations, we heard her mentor's name numerous times. He had helped many people in his 17 years of experience in the health industry. We were both curious about him and how he had impacted so many. Our counselor had transformed herself from being 22kgs overweight to an ideal body weight by following instructions from her mentor's videos and health seminars.

We were eager to meet him. He had also first remoulded himself mentally and physically 17 years back, and then started helping others. He is an

Meet our Mentor

author, certified dietician, and a physician. We requested our health counselor if we could meet her mentor. She told us to attend his health seminars. I had heard about different types of seminars but this was something new for the both of us, so we decided to go for it.

We were getting better at dealing with people and their health issues and building our little circle of influence, while doing our respective jobs. We received good appreciation from our parents and relatives. We realized that we were doing a great job by helping people transform themselves physically and mentally.

During this helpful process we got a lot of experience in handling people's problems. Our counselor helped us a great deal during the initial stage. One day she called us to her office and gave us an invitation to her mentor's health seminar. We were both very excited. She told us that our waiting period was over and we would soon get to meet the man who had influenced so many lives.

At the seminar we were both extremely impressed by his personality and the many followers. He spoke about the many people around us who were suffering from health issues and about those who have the golden chance to help them in terms of their physical and mental transformation. We realized that we needed to do something for our society and family members. Our health counselor was also 22kgs overweight once, but now she was helping others with the support of her result.

Meet our Mentor

Meghana and I also followed all necessary steps and got good results, physically and mentally.

We decided to follow this healthy lifestyle and also decided to help others. It was our choice to help others. There are many people who transformed themselves and are now living a good healthy lifestyle

We started in the year 2014 and by 2015 we had helped many people change their mental and physical health. We received many blessings from the society for doing a good job.

In our health transformation we used health supplements which are also as good as any other food to maintain oneself. (This should be added in your weight transformation) Health supplements are a boon to the health and fitness industry. Maintaining a busy lifestyle is difficult and that has led to unhealthy eating habits. Most of us eat whatever is available close at hand in order to survive. Eating is much more than just surviving, but it should also be something that satisfies the soul. Also, remember that health supplements are supportive in nature and shouldn't replace your daily food intake. Some of the most common health supplements are meal replacers, vitamin and mineral tablets, and omega 3 capsules.

Benefits of consuming health supplements are:

1. Helps meet daily requirements.
2. Improves immune system and boosts growth and repair.
3. Helps to maintain energy levels throughout the day.
4. Prevents macronutrient and micronutrient deficiencies.

9

Career opportunity

(I would like to mention that everything mentioned in the book was a voluntary decision taken by me and my wife, Meghana. It was our dream to help others after undergoing body transformation in our initial days. We both used health supplements to maintain our selves and today we are helping people with the help of proper diet, organic food supplements, positive affirmations and bach flower remedies, which help in mental and physical detoxification very effectively. 'Livewell - Lead Meaningful Life,' itself speaks of how we changed ourselves and helped others to choose a healthy lifestyle.)

As I said previously, we both started to help others in our family and friend circle while maintaining our full-time jobs and we both were very happy to do so. During this process, we also started to earn from our counseling services. And we were happy to do this work because we chose it and nobody forced us to do this.

Then through an online survey we both learnt of the huge requirement for health counselors, because in our country more than 70% of the people are suffering from lifestyle diseases due to wrong food habits. We found a big gap in counseling in the health industry. I remember that when I was a kid there was only one gym in our area, but now in the last 15 years, many health clubs, yoga centers, and gyms have been established. Around seven jogger's parks have been built in our area. So you can easily understand the necessity of health counselors.

A survey article that I read said that India is the diabetic capital of the world, and more than 50% of the cases are of type 2 diabetes, i.e., lifestyle related. Obesity is now a big issue in our country.

I also want to say thank you to our counselor and her mentor (he is our mentor also) who made us realize that there is a big need of counselors in the health industry. So we decided to grab this opportunity, but the question was how to do this. Both of us were doing jobs in private firms and were confused about jumping into this field. Our counselor asked us if we really wanted to do it and we said yes.

Career opportunity

Meghana and I discussed with each other and came to one final decision. I decided to quit my established job of 10 years for this new health industry opportunity and we decided to start counseling in January 2016.

Our counselor guided us every single step of the way. Ever since the beginning, all my clients have received 100 percent results in their transformation journey.

Meghana too chose the health industry and in April 2016, she resigned from her established job, after working for nine years, and started working with me. From 1st May 2016, Meghana joined me in our office and we both started our new career hand in hand, with the mission to change people's lives physically and mentally.

10

Formation of the Company

Livewell Fitness Solutions LLP.

Starting a company was a very bold decision. Our aim is to provide valuable services to our clients. We started different value-added services for our clients to receive better results — affirmation therapy, customized diet plan, physical and mental fitness, bach flower remedies, and organic food supplements. We also started our own free health seminar to spread awareness among the people about healthy living. We started spreading information about how to use simple methods to stay physically and mentally fit. The response we received from our seminars was very good. People began to follow the tips and started our health programmes, inspired by our own results. People were also impressed by our value-added services.

Formation of the Company

We started offering multiple services to our clients under the banner of our company 'Livewell Fitness Solutions LLP'. Our name is self-explanatory. That's why people are so attached to our counseling solutions.

We have our own office where people get multiple services under one roof. Our main goal is to bring 'Health, Wealth and Happiness' into people's lives. As I said, we also started Free Health Seminars about health awareness for a healthy lifestyle. Maintaining the body is very simple, I always tell my clients, that they come here to meet me for personal counseling, means they are almost 50% convinced to change themselves and find a proper solution for their own transformation. For example, if you are 10kgs overweight, it usually takes around three months to reduce it and then we will tell you how to maintain the weight with simple healthy steps.

I want to give the example of our mobile phones. Every day we charge it for continued and better performance. If you do not charge the phone properly, it will automatically shut down. If you want to manage this properly then your mobile must be charged every day. But after a few months or a year you feel that you should buy a new mobile with better features.

The same can be said about our bodies. We cannot change our aging bodies, but we can manage it with proper water intake, protein, vitamins, minerals, and fiber. Like the charger is the basic need of a mobile phone, our body has a few basic needs in order to maintain energy levels throughout the day. You cannot replace body parts like gadgets. You have to maintain them throughout your life or you will suffer from diseases that are related to your lifestyle. You can change everything in this world but you cannot change your body and the organs.

I want to tell you why our weight increases? Why someone becomes obese? The answer lies with you. Think about your daily routine, of the last 6 months or the last year. Are you getting 7 to 8 hours of sleep? Are you taking in proper food on time? Are you doing any exercise? Is your water intake distributed well throughout the day?

Find out the answers and you will automatically realize what has happened? How the weight was gained?

If you are overweight or obese, then you need to take care of it and in at least 6 months your body will become healthy and fit. But if you do not follow correct procedure, then you will gain even more. Maintaining the body is a lifelong job, till death. If

Formation of the Company

you ignore it now, it will automatically take you towards the hospital at a very early age. This is the time to maintain your body in a proper way with very low investment. I speak of this to all my clients till they realize that everything is in their hands and anything is possible if you are ready to change yourself.

Don't wait for a realization to hit you. Your body keeps giving signals, acknowledge them. There is no right or wrong time to get fit. The key is to stay fit, always.

Here I want to say that if you are committed to turn your life around, then you are definitely on the right path because as a counselor we know that the procedure and the path to success are easier if you want to transform yourself. We can guide you; all you have to do is hold our hands till you achieve your target.

Diet plans:

Many people raised questions about the time after the weight transformation. As a counselor we plan out our client's schedule and give them simple dietary tips. It includes exercise, water intake, and proper nutrition. We explain the whole schedule in a very simple way.

Here I want to share with you one of our clients' example who started his programme with us. During his initial days he realized that it was going to be difficult for him to follow the procedure. When someone starts the programme with us, the first thing we do is share our contact details so that he/she can easily co-ordinate with any one of us. When you start the body transformation programme, it takes some time to accept the rules and ways. I always say to my clients that they should watch the transformation for at least 3 months very carefully.

For example, if you buy a new mobile phone then it takes a few days to understand all the advanced functions. The same way, when we change our whole body, we must allow some adjustment time to the body.

The most important thing for us was to divert our client's negativity and make him/her follow the programme. As counselors we did our job perfectly. We explained to our client to simply practice good habits; change is always difficult in the initial days. Then we explained that if he/she was ready to do the body transformation, then there should not be any worry about the end results. As counselors it is our duty to provide strong moral support. When the client gets confident in his/her mind and body, he/she helps himself to become better. Here he/she consciously starts making efforts for the mind and body transformation with our guidance.

When any client starts his/her programme, we push him/her to stick with it for the first three months so that he/she can adjust to the change from inside and outside. We give a lot of motivation to our clients to stay on the road of body transformation. We always give them positive health affirmations to stay in a positive state throughout this process. Our counselor did the same thing with Meghana when she was doing her programme. With the help of this support, our clients easily follow nature's rule in order to stay fit every day.

In my view, diet means a change in one's eating habits. Our body becomes overweight because of irregular eating, less sleep, less water intake, or less or no exercise. So we always explain to our clients that we must follow the simple steps we learned in our school days but failed to follow after growing up. It is so easy to shift to healthy foods, especially for your own health.

Then the client easily understands that he/she needs to change their eating habits. And if he/she will change it in a proper way then he/she can also live a healthy lifestyle. Time is an important part of life and transformation. We do everything on time, which is essential in our day-to-day lives. But when we are totally focused on our profession, somewhere we lose our attention to maintain our self and our health, and that's when people become sick. The same situation happened with Meghana and me, but we decided to change ourselves and the change was easy because we firmly believed in it and took small steps towards it.

In our everyday lives we do all the things routinely and get appreciation also for the same. We

Formation of the Company

often forget that health appreciation is also important. You have to balance yourself in both the professional and personal arenas. Health always comes first because it is our most precious wealth.

> **When you ignore health, it will ignore you. Your body's a temple and should be worshipped. Honour it and serve it the best.**

So in our food habit plan, we first help the clients to detoxify and rid them of old constrained thoughts about weight reduction. And both of us, as counselors, strongly believe in the mental diet before starting the transformation programme. So when anybody comes to us for their 1st counseling session, we find out the reason behind this — why he/she wants to transform himself/herself? Then we proceed to questions about lifestyle.

Affirmation Therapy:

I want to share an experience of affirmation therapy during our weight management programme. One client, who joined the programme to reduce her excess weight, got amazing results during her body transformation process. But the journey was hard because of her inbuilt belief system. She tried many methods to reduce her excess weight before she came to us for counseling. I told her not to worry even if her past experiences were unsuccessful, instead to be happy that she had come to us for counseling; which meant she was ready for the physical change. It strongly indicated that there was a strong belief somewhere in her mind to undergo transformation.

If there hadn't been any hope in her, she would have never come to us. When I told her this she was so impressed and she started her story, how she had approached many weight management programmes. She had used all methods in her capacity, but after reducing some weight she had lost her confidence and had started to gain weight again. Therefore she never continued at one place for more than 2 to 3 months. She was already 30kgs overweight. After listening to her each, the first question I asked her was why she wanted to reduce the weight. Within a second she replied, 'I want relief. Because of this excess weight I am suffering from many health issues — acidity, low immunity — at the age of just 34 years.' I got a clear idea about her problem.

Then I consulted her as per our process and showed her our results and some of our clients' results. She was convinced, but I realized that she just convinced her mind to try with Livewell, as she had done many times. Then I asked her, how many kilos she wanted to reduce? She replied that if she could successfully reduce 15kgs, she would be the happiest. She couldn't bear the pain of the excess 30kgs.

First I assured her of the reduction of the 15kgs and then I gave her affirmations to prepare her mind for the same. She was confused the first time when I told her to do this activity for at least 21 days without any break. Your brain should accept that you can successfully do the mental and physical transformation. I gave her affirmations because I did not want her to go into a negative phase. We followed up with her every alternate day to find out if she was doing it or not.

And unbelievably, after just 7 days she called Meghana and told her that she was feeling much better because of the positive affirmations and that she was doing her activity regularly without any failure.

Here I want to share one thing, we changed her belief system that helped in the physical and mental transformation. She started believing that it was easy and anybody could do it even if he/she had failed before. Positive affirmations have such a strong impact on your brain that it automatically makes you believe that it is possible for you. For these affirmations you have to consciously train your brain to work on the command that you give on a daily basis.

If you typed the letter A on the keyboard then the screen will display A, not any other letter. Our brain also works on the same principle and these affirmations are nothing but a command as given on the keyboard. If your mind says it is possible to accept it as it is, then it will; and one more thing, our brain do not process any command on its own, you have to give a positive command consciously to improve your mental and physical health. So do not let any negative command influence your brain; only positive commands get you positive results.

It's an investment or expense:

I want to share one more example —one of our client's was 15kgs overweight when she walked into our office. I asked her my first question, why do you want to reduce your weight? She immediately answered that she couldn't walk continuously for more than 10 minutes. With a family wedding coming up, she had to give her 100% as there would be a lot of running around during the ceremony. She wanted her work to come off effectively and easily. Then in the course of my conversation with her, I told her that a wedding was a great time to transform herself. Her family had invested a lot to make this wedding as grand as possible. She had also bought some jewellery and clothes for herself.

I explained to her about the result very briefly, and I told her it is possible to transform the body in 3 months, but she would have to make extra efforts. When she was already to go ahead with the weight reduction, she asked me about the cost. So I explained the entire package to her. 'It's very costly sir,' she replied. I asked her only one question, 'Can you tell me, madam, the cost of health?' She couldn't say anything. So I asked her in a different way, 'How much can you invest in your health, to look healthy?'

She said that she was ready to invest, but wanted to know the procedure after the programme? So I told her in very simple words that when we become unhealthy we invest in a doctor's visit, go to the hospital for regular check-ups and buy medicines. When we want to live healthy we invest in a gym membership, good and healthy diet, and sometimes in a personal trainer who can help us. Then I asked her if she had calculated this investment before in your life? She replied, 'I have already invested a lot of money on my health issues.'

Then I asked her if she had felt at any point that this was a costly method? She said, 'No. It was my body's need and so I wanted to become healthy, that's the reason why I spent money on it.' Later on I asked her, if weight reduction was a priority in the current situation. She replied by saying, 'Yes, today it is an urgent need for me; I have already suffered from so many physical issues because of excess weight.'

So, I made her understand, without forcing the issue, how important it was to work on her weight. If not, there would be troubles in the future by default. Spending money today would automatically prevent expenditure later on. We don't even blink when it comes to spending huge amounts on a wedding, but our first wealth is our own health. Good health is also an essential part of our lives. It didn't matter where she wanted to do the programme, but this investment is paramount. At Livewell we take these charges for our services because we both know what it is to go through it. We have reduced our weight and have already given many people successful results. Other service providers are also doing the same thing but only packages are different. In the end, the goal is the same. So she should invest wisely in her health. Eating healthy can cost money but eating unhealthy, low-cost food can cost one's own life. If she wanted to celebrate her memorable health goal, then she should invest wisely.

She was happy and satisfied with the explanation. She grasped the meaning of my reasoning and was ready to do the mental and physical transformation with under our guidance.

The point is that, we spend a lot of money on many things without any questions. When it comes down to our own health, then we start comparing it with other costs. But if you link these investments with the ultimate result, you will understand why it is important today than afterwards.

Exercise and Meditation:

I would like to share another client example. For good health, you must do 1hour of exercise, have proper 7 to 8 hours of sleep, drink a minimum of 3 liters of water, and have proper food intake every day. This must be done throughout one's life for balanced living. But somewhere in our routine, we fail to follow these things properly and then end up being overweight, obese or underweight.

One of my clients' who was following some of the steps, could not do so regularly because he was working in a corporate office. He could not manage enough time for the exercise and he spent around 10 hours a day at his sedentary job. After he started the health programme with us we told him the importance of a healthy lifestyle. If you failed to follow any one of the activities' during the day, then it would not provide the expected end result. We demonstrated some exercises that he could do at home.

His daily schedule was like this —day started at 6 a.m.; watched news channels, read the newspaper

Formation of the Company

and checked mobile messages; left for work around 8 a.m.. So I told him that he needed to pull out a little bit time in these two hours for his own health; to do simple exercises or to just walk. I explained to him that the activities he was indulging in were of no benefit to his body. It had unfortunately become a part of his life. He tried to say that from newspapers and the news we gained information about what was happening around us. I said I agreed with him, but what about his health. If his focus was on outside events, who was going to attend his body and health. Mobile messages could always be checked on the way to the workplace. I reassured him that he did not have to let go of everything, but manage things as per his work schedule.

Out of a 10 hours' workday, he needed to take out some time for his health; to be fit for his profession too. His work was sedantry, and to lose 20kgs, he would have to move his body a lot. Health is more important than the other things. So I told him to start off by trying to take out 15 minutes for exercise or just a basic walk, and then gradually increase the exercise. His office was located on the 3rd floor, so I urged him to begin by taking the stairs till the 1st floor and then use the lift. After a few days he should only use the staircase. Later on, I also taught him some office exercises which he could do during office hours. We discussed his performance in the monthly one-on-one meetings

In the entire world, everyone has 24 hours in a day; it depends on the person how he/she utilizes this given time. That's why our main focus during the counseling sessions is for our respected client to realize that they can achieve their goals with easy and simple steps.

We also help people with meditation. We tell our client to sit for at least 15 minutes each day, in silence, before going to sleep and concentrate on their breathing and try to see the end result and feel that result in the body. Many people watch TV before turning in, while many read mobile messages before sleep. We always advise our clients to reduce and eventually stop these habits for the body and mind to experience good results. So before sleeping if you provide some positive input to your mind, it will help you throughout your life. Always go to sleep early, avoid watching TV and checking mobile phones. In the initial days it will be difficult but you have to push yourself consciously and as counselors, we are always ready to help you in every difficult situation. If you want to become a good performer in your life then you have to adapt to good habits, which will help you to perform well in your personal and professional life.

Finally you become disciplined:

I would like to share my experience about how I became disciplined towards good physical and mental health. Let me tell you one thing, if I can do this then so can you; if I could become disciplined, then you can also become the same. It requires conscious efforts to do the good things. First the ideas come to our brain and then they gradually appear physically.

If I say you need to do regular exercise, take in proper nutrition, adequate amount of water, 7 to 8 hours of sound sleep, then you must do these things for your own health, consciously. I can understand that when you start, you will face obstacles, but you have to cross those old mind barriers for the betterment of your own mental and physical health. As I said earlier, everyone has 24 hours in a day, so think about how some people are successful and healthy in this world. Can nature give them extra hours a day to achieve their goals? No, not at all. Everybody has 24 hours a day, so if some can achieve their target, then what stops you from reaching yours.

Discipline is key. And if you want to become successful in your personal and professional life then you need to follow nature's rule, i.e., regular exercise, sound sleep, adequate water and good nutritional food throughout your life. Your personal habits always reflect in your day-to-day routine. First, health is your wealth, rest of the things are secondary. In the morning, after your 7 to 8 hours of sound sleep, you need to do some exercise, and then eat a healthy breakfast, then a proper homemade lunch, and in the evening a small snack. Throughout your day drink a minimum of 3 liters of water. This change doesn't happen overnight and requires conscious efforts.

History is witness that bad things are more easily adopted than the good things. But I want to say that if you do good things consciously then your future will be bright. Your brain and mind will work in sync with your good habits, and for these good habits, as a counselor, we are always ready to help you. Here I want you to know that when I was 84kgs I was particular in my professional work, like timely reporting to higher authorities, but not much in my personal life — like irregular eating habits, less amount of water, late night meals, 6 hours of sleep. This made me gain the extra 20kgs.

Formation of the Company

Then at one point I realized that I was very punctual in my professional life but not in my personal life. When I realized this I started to follow my wife who reduced her extra 19kgs in 5 months. I followed all the things in a proper way. That is when I realized why it is so important to follow the good habits. I started all the right things consciously in my personal life. If your health is poor then what is the meaning of earning money? Then gradually I became disciplined in my personal life and my body was transformed from 84kgs to 64kgs in just 6 months. As I said earlier, anybody can do this. Meghana reduced her 19kgs in 5 months. It is very easy to reduce the excess weight. We will help you make it possible. For things to change, you need to change ~ Mr. Jim Rohn. Always maintain yourself with your ideal weight then you will not suffer from any lifestyle-related diseases.

We will help you to maintain your reduced weight throughout your life. Once it is reduced then it becomes very easy to maintain because you have already come to know the procedure of a healthy lifestyle. It is so simple and joyful to lead a healthy life. Become a disciplined person in your personal life, then automatically you will become disciplined in your professional life. Your coming generations will also live healthy.

After completing our education, we need to struggle to find work. Similarly, when you are getting ready to change yourself, your mind and body also need to struggle in order to adapt to new things. Initially, it will be difficult but later on it will become a habit. If you compare this with your profession, which takes around 2 to 3 years, you require only 6 months to 1 year to transform yourself.

Think about it!

Be Healthy, Be Happy.

Formation of the Company

Conclusion:

I would like to conclude by saying that you should not wait for someone to bring a change in you, but become the change yourself. I was reluctant to change but my wife wasn't. Ultimately, she convinced me to change, but it would've been better if I had convinced myself to do that. After founding Livewell Fitness Solutions LLP, we always try our best to help others transform, but that is only possible if you want to change from within.

Inner peace and outer health both work together hand in hand. Our biggest dream is to help people undergo a mind and body transformation and we will chase it till it's done. Only a yes from you can make a huge difference. In the end, we will be happy, but you will be the one who'll experience the greatest happiness. Give it a thought, an opportunity. Give yourself a chance, and move towards transforming yourself.

11

Our services

- Consulting about healthy lifestyle
- Exercise and Mediation
- Customize diet plan
- Affirmation therapy
- Physical and Mental detoxification
- Organic food supplements
- Bach flower remedies (For controlling emotions)
- DMIT Test (To know your hidden talent with fingerprints)

Contact/Whatsapp number —

9967225349 / 9702277597

Email —

livewellmumbai@gmail.com

Website —

www.livewellfitnesssolutions.com

Facebook page —

https://www.facebook.com/LivewellFitnessSolutions/

Facebook Closed Group —

https://www.facebook.com/groups/LivewellHealthFitnessDiet/

Author Bios

Sanket Prasade has a Diploma in Electrical Engg., and is a BSc. graduate in Industrial Science. Sanket Prasade is the founding owner of Livewell Fitness Solutions LLP. Sanket's excess weight motivated him to become fit, ultimately leading him to leave his established job and chase his dream to help other people become fit. Now, he is a Master Trainer certified by NIESBUD Govt. of India, he is certified NLP practitioner, Reiki practitioner, and an affirmation therapist. His eagerness to reach out to more people and to influence them to be healthy, motivated him to write his first book, Livewell—Lead Meaningful Life. While he is helping people get strong and fit, Sanket loves to take his family out on road trips.

Meghana Prasade is the perfect combination of a dedicated businesswoman, an affectionate wife, and a responsible and loving mother. With a Masters in chemistry, Meghana worked full-time, managing Sanket and her son and doing all her household chores.  After facing weight issues and overcoming them, she motivated her husband to do the same. This is where it all began. A few months later, with her constant support and help, her husband started Livewell Fitness Solutions LLP. Meghana works with her husband at their company office and is also a certified professional healer, Reiki practitioner, NLP practitioner, and an affirmation therapist.

www.ingramcontent.com/pod-product-compliance
Lightning Source LLC
Chambersburg PA
CBHW031637160426
43196CB00006B/459